HURRICANE VACATION

D1511600

written by Dr. Heather L. Beal
illustrated by Jasmine Mills

Much love and appreciation to my family, especially my husband, who supports me
no matter what the weather brings.

Leileiana and Nickolai, as always, I love you both and thank you for being there
to teach me how to be a better person.

For all the children out there, I want to tip the odds in YOUR favor. I hope this book
helps you become stronger through reading. – Heather

TRAIN 4 SAFETY PRESS BREMERTON, WA

Text and illustrations copyright © 2019 by Heather L. Beal. All rights reserved. Except as
permitted under the United States Copyright Act of 1976, no part of this book may be
reproduced, stored in or introduced into a retrieval system or transmitted, in any form, or
by any means (electronic or mechanical, photocopying, recording, or otherwise), without
the prior written permission of both the copyright owner and the publisher of this book.

ISBN 978-1-9476901-1-0 (paperback)
ISBN 978-1-9476901-2-7 (hardback)
ISBN 978-1-9476901-3-4 (e-book)

Library of Congress Control Number: 2019916540

<u>Other Publications by Train 4 Safety Press</u>

Elephant Wind

Tummy Rumble Quake

Lions, Leopards, and Storms, Oh My!

<u>We Love Reviews!</u>
If you have read our books - please provide a review on sites like Amazon, Barnes & Nobles, GoodReads, or wherever else you purchase your books from. Reviews help draw attention to these books and others like it.
Your Opinion Really Does Matter!

<u>A NOTE TO THE READER</u>
The information in this book is meant to supplement response protocols and is therefore provided 'as is' without warranty of any kind, neither implied nor expressed, including but not limited to implied warranties of suitability for a particular purpose. Train 4 Safety Press, the writers, editors, illustrators and designers of this work shall in no event be liable for damages or losses including, without limitation, direct, indirect,special, punitive, incidental or consequential damages resulting from or caused by this book or its content, including without limitation, any error, omission, or defect. In any event, liability shall not exceed the retail price, or any lesser amount actually paid for the purchase of this book.

"Dinner," called Aunt Sarah.

Niko jumped up, sending sand everywhere. "Whoo-hoo!"

"They just issued a hurricane watch." Uncle Brian said as he sat down.

"Hurricane?" Niko asked, "What's that?"

"A hurricane is a big storm-," began Aunt Sarah.

"GI-NORMOUS," said Emma.

Lily frowned. "We don't have hurricanes at home."

"That's right Lily. Hurricanes form over tropical waters, like the ocean," explained Aunt Sarah.

"A watch means it could be here in a few days."

Lily couldn't stop thinking about the hurricane as she brushed her teeth. "Isn't a hurricane like a thunderstorm?"

"Hurricanes are much bigger," said Aunt Sarah.

"They can cover hundreds of miles. Because they're so big, they can bring more rain, stronger winds, and even flooding."

Niko ran down the hall.

"Lily, Lily, guess what? Uncle Brian said we can help hurricane-roof the house tomorrow!"

"Hurricane-proof Niko," chuckled Uncle Brian.

"They just upgraded to a hurricane warning," Uncle Brian said. "They're recommending evacuation."

Aunt Sarah nodded. "I just got a text, they want me at the hospital tonight."

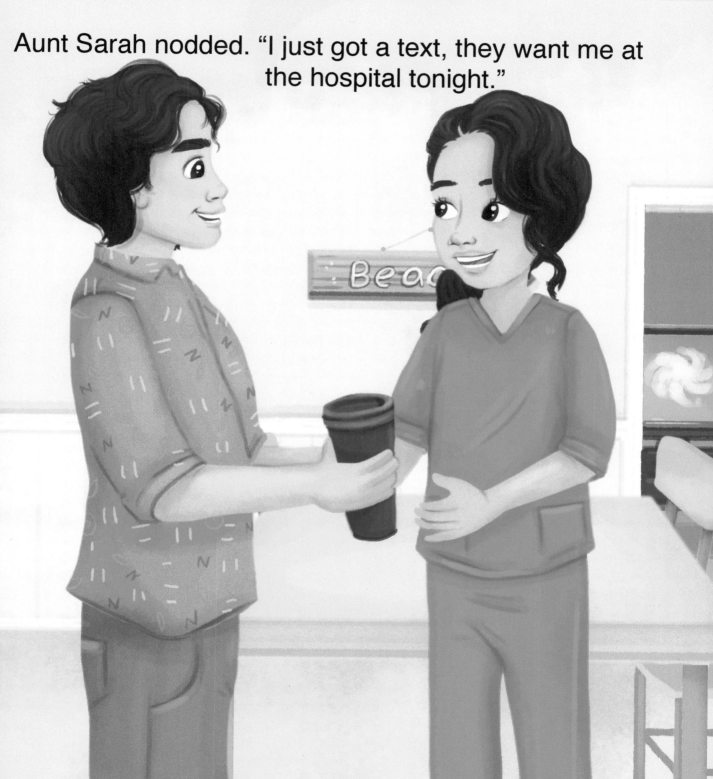

"What's e-vac-u-late-ion?" asked Niko.

"E-vac-u-ation," corrected Lily.

"It means to get away from the storm, or go somewhere safer, like a shelter," said Aunt Sarah.

"I think that's everything," said Emma as she and Lily put the last of the outdoor toys in the garage.

"What are they doing?"
Lily asked.

"Covering the windows
so they can't break
during the storm."

"Uncle Brian said we're going to the shelter after dinner," said Niko as he dropped the bucket of nails he was carrying with a thump.

"What's a shelter?"

"A shelter," said Emma, "is a strong building, like a school or church, where we'll be safest during the storm."

"But your mom isn't coming with us," said Lily. "She'll be ok. Doctors stay at the hospital to help. Mom did that last time," Emma said confidently.

"Mom taught me a song about shelters," said Emma.

"Do you want to hear it?"

The kids nodded.

"The hurricane's a- coming stay or go?

A shelter is the safest place you know,

There's lots of families there, and maybe some pets too.

Just look for the helpers, they'll help you."

Emma smiled. "We'll be there together, and we'll help each other. That's the most important thing."

Uncle Brian looked up as rain started pounding against the roof. "We're going to see lots of rain and wind before the eye of the hurricane gets here."

"Eye?" asked Niko. "Hurricanes have eyes?
That's so cool!"

"The eye is the storm center," Uncle Brian explained. "When it passes over, it may seem like the storm's over, but it's really only half over."

"It's important to listen to weather reports to know for sure."

"Everyone packed? It's time to go."

"I packed clothes for Emma, me, and Niko," said Lily.

"I got the story books and toys," said Emma.

Niko ran out of the room. "Where's Dino?" he yelled.

"Who?" asked Uncle Brian.

"Dino is Niko's stuffed frog," explained Lily.

"Niko," began Uncle Brian, "We need to go.
Dino will be ok."

"No!
Not without Dino!"

"Where did you last see Dino," Lily asked.

"Dino helped me and Uncle Brian with the windows."

"Emma, you and Lily go look in the garage," directed Uncle Brian.

"Niko and I will look around here."

Suddenly, the lights flickered and went out.

"It's ok," Uncle Brian said calmly and handed out flashlights.

"We'll find him Niko." Lily squeezed his hand.

"Don't worry."

A few minutes later Lily and Emma came running back, flashlights bobbing in the dark.

"He was in the nail bucket!"
Emma giggled.

"Dino!" shrieked Niko as the lights came back on.

"We're family," said Lily smiling, "We help each other."

"Are we ready now?"
asked Uncle Brian.

Niko grinned.

"I'm going to take good care
of Dino at the shelter."

"He's part of my family too and we're all going to be ok because we'll be together."

Questions and Activities from Lily and Niko:

Questions:

1. What is the difference between a hurricane watch and a hurricane warning?

2. What does evacuation mean? Where would you go?

3. How should you prepare you home for a hurricane?

4. What should be in your "ready bag?"

Activities:

1. Talk to your parents about the plan. Where would you do if a hurricane watch/warning was issued? Where would you go if an evacuation order was given?

2. Practice singing the Hurricane Vacation song so you know what to do. (Sung to the tune of "She'll be Coming Round the Mountain").

3. Prepare a "ready bag."

Resources:

Here are a few sites where you can learn more about being ready....

1. https://www.ready.gov/kids

2. https://www.cdc.gov/disasters/index.html

3. https://www.acf.hhs.gov/ohsepr

4. Your local (county / state) emergency management office

Ready Tots and Resources:

Congratulations on learning about hurricane preparedness! Check out our webpage www.train4safety.com/ready-tots/ to print out a certificate of training completion and to get more references on how to stay safe.

CPSIA information can be obtained
at www.ICGtesting.com
Printed in the USA
BVHW090441181119
564038BV00004B/36/P